To Open, or Not To Open

Featuring the Rule of 20

Marty Bergen

Bergen Books

Bergen Books
9 River Chase Terrace
Palm Beach Gardens, FL 33418-6817

First Edition published 2003.
Printed in the United States of America.
10 9 8 7 6 5 4 3 2 1

First Printing: July, 2003

Library of Congress Control Number: 2001012345

ISBN 0-9716636-88

Dedication

*In memory of
all the good people who were
tragically and senselessly
taken from us
on 9/11/01.*

Bridge Books by Marty Bergen

Better Rebidding with Bergen

Hand Evaluation: Points, Schmoints!

Understanding 1NT Forcing

Marty Sez

Marty Sez...Volume 2

POINTS SCHMOINTS!

More POINTS SCHMOINTS!

Introduction to Negative Doubles

Negative Doubles

Better Bidding with Bergen, Volume I

Better Bidding with Bergen, Volume II

Everyone's Guide to the New Convention Card

Thanks To:

Layout, cover design, and editing by
Hammond Graphics.

My very special thanks to:
Cheryl Angel, Cheryl Bergen, Gary Blaiss,
Trish and John L. Block, Ollie Burno, Caitlin,
Nancy Deal, Pete Filandro, Jim Garnher, Terry Gerber,
Lynn and Steve Gerhard, Steve Jones, Doris Katz,
Al Kimel, Danny Kleinman, Alex Martelli,
Harriet and David Morris, Phyllis Nicholson,
Mary and Richard Oshlag, Helene Pittler, Dave Porter,
David Pollard, Mark Raphaelson, Jesse Reisman,
John Rudy, Eric Sandberg, Maggie Sparrow,
Tom Spector, Merle Stetser, and Bobby Stinebaugh.

Coming Attractions

Books by Marty

Marty Sez ... Volume 3
More brand-new hints with an easy-to-read format.
Each tip begins with a concise, practical "what's it all
about," followed by a helpful explanation and
instructive examples. You will learn:
   When should a defender win his ace of trumps?
   When *not* to use the honor from the short side first.
   When to preempt despite having an opening bid.
   And a whole lot more.

Softcover books – under $10

No Mercy - Attack Their Redouble
How to make life difficult for your opponents.

Making the Most of Third Seat
When to open light, when to preempt, and when to go
quietly and pass.

**For information on ordering books
and CDs from Marty,
please refer to pages 60-64.
GREAT DISCOUNTS!**

To order, call
1-800-386-7432
or email: mbergen@mindspring.com

Contents

Part I - Evaluating Whether to Open

Section 1: In the Beginning
The Rule of 20 – What's the Story?... 10
FYI 11
When Experts Ignore the Rule of 20 12-14
Rule of 20 Q&A 15-17

Section 2: Upgrading and Downgrading
Good and Bad Honors 18
Honors in Short Suits 19
Quick Tricks 20
Happy Together 21
Appreciating Intermediates 22-23
Very Happy Together 24
Your Other Suits 25
6-4 is Worth More 26
Too Strong to Open Three 27
Evaluating Summary 28
The Rule of 22 29
Tiebreakers for Borderline Hands 30

Section 3: Your Turn to Shine
Quiz - Open or Not 31-34
Quiz - Preempt or Not 35-38

Part II - After Deciding to Open

Setting the Scene 41

Which Suit Should You Open? 42-44

Limiting Your Hand 45

Rebidding After Finding a Fit 46

Competitive Bidding Guidelines 47-48

To Bid, or Not to Bid? 49-57

Also Worth Noting 58

Responder - Easy Does it 59

Recommended Books and CDs 60-64

Rule of 20 – What's the Story?

Why is the Rule of 20 so necessary?

It provides an easy but accurate method to determine if your hand is worth an opening bid. Many players do not count short suits before a fit is found, and only add for length if they have a suit(s) with at least five cards. With fewer than 13 HCP and no long suit, these players pass some worthwhile hands that *should* be opened. "Length players" would pass hands like the following:

♠ K Q 5 4   ♡ A 8 7 3   ◇ 6   ♣ K 10 6 4
(12 HCP + 0 for length totals only 12).

Because the Rule of 20 takes suits of less than five cards into account, opening this promising hand is a snap.

When do you apply it?

In first or second seat, when unsure whether or not to open a borderline hand. It is not relevant in third or fourth seat.

What do you do?

Add the length of your two longest suits to your HCP. On the hand above, 12 HCP + 4 spades + 4 hearts = 20.

What then?

If the total is 20 or more, open the bidding. Use your normal criteria in deciding which suit to bid. With fewer than 20, either pass, or preempt (with a nice long suit).

FYI

1. Using numbers and hyphens to signify distribution:
In this book, I will always use numbers and hyphens to indicate the general distribution of the hand. The long suits will be designated first. For example, "5-5-2-1" shows a hand containing two 5-card suits, a doubleton and a singleton. It says nothing about which are the 5-card suits.

"6-4" or "5-5" will always refer to the two longest suits, not necessarily spades and hearts.

2. Defining "open:"
In this book, "open" means "at the 1 level." Because I am not concerned with 1NT openings, I will always be referring to "one of a suit."

3. Keep in mind:
This book deals with Rule of 20 hands held by the potential opening bidder. The hand evaluation guidelines that follow also apply to hands of *any* strength for *any* player.

4. Which suit of equal length is used to add up to 20?
In reality, it makes no difference. For consistency, I will always use the higher-ranking one(s). For example, to decide whether or not this hand meets the Rule of 20:

♠ A 9 7 6 5 4   ♡ 3   ◇ K J 6   ♣ K 4 3

I add: 11 HCP + 6 spades + 3 diamonds = 20.

5. Vulnerability for bidding decisions:
On all hands *in this book*, I suggest taking the same action whether vulnerable or not.

Do Experts Follow The Rule of 20?

Only sometimes. How well do they fare when they prefer to rely on their own judgment? You be the judge. Here are some examples from high-level tournament play.

♠ 9   ♡ A 10 8 2   ◊ A 10   ♣ Q 10 8 5 4 2

In the Women's Team Trials, a world champion held this hand as dealer with both sides vulnerable. She passed, which seemed very wrong to me with such an obvious Rule of 20 hand. The auction continued:

Our Heroine	West	North	East
Pass!	1◊	Pass	1♠
2♣	2♠	3♣	4♠
5♣	Pass	Pass	Dbl
All Pass			

Do I agree with the eventual 5♣ bid? No. **Too many players, including experts, sacrifice too often in five of a minor**. Unless you have 11 trumps or once-in-a-lifetime distribution, **on most hands, the five level belongs to the opponents**.

Why did our heroine bid 5♣? She realized how good her hand was, especially once she found a fit. She didn't expect to make 5♣, but hoped to lose less than the opponents would have scored in 4♠.

How did she do? She went down two doubled, for a loss of 500 points. That would have been less expensive than 4♠ making four, a duplicate score of 620.

Unfortunately, the opponents had no chance to make 4♠. The decision to sacrifice in 5♣ cost her team dearly.

What happened when the opposing team played this deal? The sensible player who held these cards opened 1♣ and was subsequently able to rebid that suit. Because she had already given her partner a good description of her hand, she didn't have to guess at a high level.

Did you get the message? Regardless of your experience and ability, describing your hand ASAP makes life easier. Once you have told your story, you can sit back and leave the decisions to partner.

The next example is taken from the Spingold Master Knockout Teams. Once again, the perpetrator was the dealer, this time with favorable vulnerability. If you admired South's distribution in the previous example, this one will knock your socks off:

$$♠ — \quad ♡ 6 \quad ♢ K J 10 9 6 5 2 \quad ♣ A J 10 9 7$$

12 cards in two suits – I haven't seen very many of those! The Rule of 20 resolves all doubts: 9 HCP + 7 (diamonds) + 5 (clubs) totals 21. In addition, I absolutely *love* the minor-suit intermediates. Without question, I would have opened 1♢.

This hand was played at four tables, and I'd like to focus on the two auctions where the experts attempted to describe this hand with an initial pass! Were they able to catch up?

South	West	North	East
Pass!	1♦	1♠	2♡
3♣	3♡	Pass	4♡
All Pass			

If you believe that South's one sign of life did justice to the cards he held, "you ain't seen nothing yet." Here is the auction produced by the world champion at another table.

South	West	North	East
Pass!	1♦	1♠	2♡
Pass	3♡	Pass	4♡
All Pass			

Wow! Despite his spectacular distribution, South never bid! This incredible display of non-bidding is exactly what he would have done holding:

♠ 4 3 2   ♡ 4 3 2   ♦ 5 4 3 2   ♣ 4 3 2

Maybe I'm crazy, but treating the 7-5 hand just like this Yarborough leaves me speechless. How did it work out? About as well as it deserved. 4♡ was laydown for 11 tricks, a score of 650. Meanwhile, 5♦ doubled would be down only one – a loss of 100. What a surprise! The 7-5 hand played better on offense than defense.

Experts and world champions have great confidence in their ability to figure out what to do at any given moment. On most hands, they do just fine. There is no way that the average player can even hope to emulate that success. However, by following the Rule of 20, you can achieve good results that are sometimes missed by more advanced players who *think* they can "pass now, and guess later."

Rule of 20 Q&A

Question: Simply adding to 20 seems too easy. Is that all there is to the Rule of 20?

Answer: Yes and no. If you use the Rule of 20 in its most basic form, you will do just fine. However, always remember that there are logical exceptions to even the best bridge "rules."

For example, take a look at this hand:

♠ Q ♡ Q J ♢ Q 5 4 3 2 ♣ Q J 4 3 2

You have 10 HCP, and two 5-card suits. That adds to 20, which "says" to open! However, with no aces or kings and three very questionable honors in your short suits, no one should even consider opening this horrible assortment of overrated queens and jacks.

At the other extreme, consider this very attractive hand:

♠ A Q 10 9 8 ♡ A 10 9 8 ♢ 10 9 8 7 ♣ —

You have "only" 10 HCP + a 5-card suit + a 4-card suit. That totals 19, which does not satify the Rule of 20. But with your great distribution, superb intermediates, length in both majors, 2½ quick tricks, and an easy rebid, opening 1♠ is clearcut.

Every bridge player must learn to upgrade attractive hands and downgrade ugly ones.

Question: If I don't feel confident about my evaluation skills, can I still use the Rule of 20?

Answer: Absolutely. Of course, improving those skills is important, and fortunately, can be done. Regardless, Marty Sez: whatever your level, don't leave home without the Rule of 20.

Question: After using the Rule of 20 to decide whether or not to open, what else should I do with the total I got by adding HCP to the length of my two longest suits?

Answer: Nothing! This "19, 20 or 21, etc." total is relevant only when deciding whether to open. Once you have made that decision, you can discard that number.

Question: If I open based on the Rule of 20, am I opening "light" or "sound?"

Answer: The Rule of 20 features "light" opening bids. This technique enables players to open distributional hands they might otherwise pass.

Question: I've been using the Rule of 20, but have had some bad results after opening light. Any suggestions?

Answer: No advice or technique is immune from some bad results. If you're uncomfortable opening light, you might decide not to open with a "so-so 20." After all, **not all 20's are created equal.**

Question: How does vulnerability affect the Rule of 20?

Answer: You can be slightly more aggressive in opening borderline hands when you are not vulnerable.

Question: When using the Rule of 20, does it matter whether I'm playing match point duplicate as opposed to rubber bridge, teams, etc.?

Answer: No; bridge is bridge. Getting in the first punch and beginning the description of your hand ASAP is *always* the best way to go.

Question: Will the Rule of 20 tell me which suit to open?

Answer: No, it won't. I will address this in detail in Part II of this book.

Question: If I open using the Rule of 20, are there any differences in how I proceed from there?

Answer: NO. Once you open the bidding, you are announcing that you have an opening bid, and will follow through and respect partner's forcing bids, just as if you had 13 HCP. Any time you open a light, distributional hand with more offense than defense, you might decide to remove partner's penalty double, depending on the auction and your particular hand.

Now that I've answered some often-asked questions, I'll show you how hand evaluation techniques can improve your Rule of 20 judgment.

Upgrading and Downgrading Honors

In the 4-3-2-1 point count, aces and tens are underrated, while queens and jacks are overrated. Kings are rated fairly.

Rank these hands from weakest to strongest based on the quality of their 12 HCP. Assign a "+" for each ace or ten, and a "−" for each queen or jack. Then decide if you consider each hand worth an opening bid.

1. ♠ K x x x   ♡ Q J x   ◇ Q J x   ♣ Q J x

2. ♠ A 10 x x   ♡ A 10 x   ◇ x x x   ♣ K J 10

3. ♠ K x x x   ♡ A x x   ◇ A x x   ♣ J 10 x

4. ♠ J x x x   ♡ Q J 10   ◇ K J x   ♣ A x x

Hand #1 is the weakest. You have 6 minuses (3 queens and 3 jacks), and no pluses. This is an easy pass.

Hand #4 is not as bad. You have 2 pluses (ace and ten), and 4 minuses (3 jacks and a queen). Too many minuses; once again, I'd pass.

Hand #3 is better. You have 3 pluses (2 aces and a ten), and 1 minus (jack). I would open.

Hand #2 is definitely the strongest. You have 5 pluses (2 aces and 3 tens), and 1 minus. An obvious opening bid.

The Short End of the Stick

Honors in short suits should be devalued.

Here are the least effective honors in short suits.
I recommend subtracting one point for each of these
holdings. I'll refer to these as "maxi-subtractions."
Singleton: king, queen, or jack   **Doubleton:** QJ, Qx, Jx

The following holdings are not as bad, but they should also
be devalued. I'll call these "mini-subtractions."
Singleton: ace   **Doubleton:** AJ, KQ, KJ

Rank these 5-5 hands from weakest to strongest based on
subtractions. Each one has 12 HCP, but would you open?

1.   ♠ Q x x x x ♡ A J ◇ K x x x x ♣ Q

2.   ♠ A Q x x x ♡ x x ◇ K Q J x x ♣ x

3.   ♠ Q x x x x ♡ Q J ◇ A x x x x ♣ K

4.   ♠ Q J x x x ♡ x x ◇ K Q x x x ♣ A

Hand # 3 is the weakest. You have 2 maxi-subtractions.
You should pass.

Hand #1 is not as bad. You have 1 maxi-subtraction and
1 mini. You should still pass.

Hand # 4 is better. You have only 1 mini-subtraction.
You should open.

Hand # 2 is the strongest. You have *no* subtractions,
and are delighted to open.

Quick Tricks

Counting quick tricks is essential for good hand evaluation.

For each suit:
$$AK = 2, \quad AQ = 1\frac{1}{2}, \quad A = 1, \quad KQ = 1, \quad Kx = \frac{1}{2}$$
(Jacks are never "quick," and the maximum per suit is two).

Counting your quick tricks helps you appreciate the power of aces and kings, and enables you to decide if you have "good points," or merely a handful of "schmoints." Count your quick tricks on every hand.

How Many Quick Tricks Do You Need?

I am often asked: "Marty, can I ever open with fewer than two quick tricks?"

My answer is, "Absolutely, positively." Would you pass any of these "fewer than 2 quick trick" hands?

♠ 6   ♡ K J 10 6 4   ◇ K Q J 9   ♣ Q J 5

♠ A J 10 6 4   ♡ K 10 2   ◇ Q J 9 8 5   ♣ —

♠ A Q J 9 6 3   ♡ Q J 10 8 5   ◇ 7   ♣ 5

Of course not. However, I am willing to say:
Most hands worth opening in first or second seat have at least two quick tricks.

Happy Together

All honor cards increase in value when combined with other honors in the same suit.

Rank these hands from weakest to strongest after adding up the quick tricks. Each hand contains 12 HCP. Once again, decide if you would open the bidding.

1. ♠ x x ♡ A Q J x ◇ K Q x x ♣ x x x

2. ♠ A x ♡ Q J x x ◇ Q x x x ♣ K x x

3. ♠ A x ♡ Q J x x ◇ K Q x x ♣ x x x

Hand #2 is the weakest.
You have 1½ quick tricks: ♠A = 1, ♣K = ½.
Three of your suits contain only one honor. Honor cards are not worth as much when they are "isolated." I would not open the bidding with this hand.

Hand #3 is a little better.
You have 2 quick tricks: ♠A = 1, ◇KQ = 1.
Because your diamond honors are "together," this hand is stronger than hand #2. Although it's only a so-so hand, most players would open, and so would I.

Hand #1 is the strongest.
You have 2½ quick tricks: ♡AQ = 1½ , ◇KQ = 1.
The same 12 HCP as the other two hands, but each of your five honor cards is "supported" by other honor cards. Opening this hand is clearcut.

Love Those Intermediates

Consider these 4-card suits, each of which contains 3 HCP.

1. K 4 3 2	2. K 9 3 2
3. K 9 8 2	4. K 9 8 7
5. K 10 3 2	6. K 10 8 2
7. K 10 8 7	8. K 10 9 8

Imagine that you are declaring a notrump contract, and dummy has J 6 5 in this suit. You have plenty of stoppers and entries in the other suits and need to develop trick(s) in this suit. How do you like your chances?

What a difference a spot (or two) can make! With the first two holdings, you have no assurance of taking even one trick, not to mention the problem of guessing the best finessing technique.

As your intermediates increase, so do your prospects. With # 3-7, you are assured of one trick, with varying chances for two, or even the possibility of three tricks with # 6 and # 7.

However, when you hold K 10 9 8, you are guaranteed to win two tricks, and will win three 50% of the time. That's my kind of suit.

In conclusion, **when considering whether or not to open the bidding, be aware of the presence or absence of intermediate cards.**

By the way: Appreciating your intermediates is necessary on virtually *all* hands, both for bidding and card play.

Arlene Adds 'Em Up

While teaching in Long Island, NY, one of my favorite students was Arlene, a lovely lady who marched to her own drummer. In class one day, Arlene thought forever before opening 1♢. Eventually, she became the dummy in 4♠. Everyone was staring at me when she tabled her hand:

♠ K 10 9 8   ♡ 2   ♢ A Q 10 9 8   ♣ 9 7 6

The surprised declarer could not control herself. "What are you doing, Arlene? How could you open with 9 HCP?"

I searched for the words to maintain peace – but I need not have worried. Arlene had the situation well in hand.

"Marty taught us that just as jacks are half as good as queens, tens are half as good as jacks – so I counted the two tens as one point. That brought me up to 10. It follows that nines are half as good as tens – ¼ of a point each; the three nines got me to 10¾. Two eights equal one nine, and that ¼ brings the total to 11. Add the 5-card suit and the 4-card suit, and this hand meets the Rule of 20!"

For the first and only time in our nine years together, every one of Arlene's friends sat in stunned silence. They turned to me, anxiously awaiting my informed rebuttal.

I firmly believe that I appreciate the value of spot cards as much as any player. However, I can honestly say that using eights as a criterion for opening was a new one on me. On the other hand, I had to admit that Arlene's arithmetic skills were beyond reproach.

"Well done, Arlene. I cannot speak for others, but I have no problem opening a hand with such lovely texture."

P.S. 4♠ made easily.

Very Happy Together

The strength of your long suit(s) is crucial.

Therefore, when honors and intermediates get together in suits of at least four cards, you've really got something.

Although each of the following 5-4-3-1 hands has two quick tricks, the trick-taking potential is quite different. Rank the hands from weakest to strongest based on the quality of the two longest suits. Also decide if you would open the bidding.

1.   ♠ 10   ♡ J 8 7 6 3   ◇ K Q J   ♣ A 9 5 4

2.   ♠ 4   ♡ A Q J 10 7   ◇ 6 5 3   ♣ K J 9 8

3.   ♠ 4   ♡ A J 9 8 3   ◇ K 7 5   ♣ Q J 10 6

Hand # 1 is the weakest. Each of your two longest suits has only one honor and one intermediate. You should pass.

Hand # 3 is better. You have five honors in hearts and clubs, and your heart intermediates are promising. Open the bidding.

Hand # 2 is the strongest. The ♣9 8 bolsters your club suit, and you love your 100 honors in hearts. In fact, Marty Sez: with a suit that contains four honors, add one point to the value of your hand. Open this hand without any reservations.

Don't Forget Your Other Suits

The Rule of 20 applies only to your two longest suits. Therefore, when deciding if you should open, it's up to you to consider the distribution of your two other suits.

Consider the following hands:

♠ 5 4 ♡ K Q 10 8 7 ◇ A J 9 6 ♣ 3 2

♠ 5 4 3 ♡ K Q 10 8 7 ◇ A J 9 6 ♣ 2

♠ 5 4 3 2 ♡ K Q 10 8 7 ◇ A J 9 6 ♣ —

Obviously, the last hand has the best distribution, and the second hand is more interesting than the first. However, when you apply the Rule of 20, the total on all three is the same 19 (10 HCP + 5 hearts + 4 diamonds).

Because the high cards and intermediates are concentrated in your long suits, all three of these are upgradable hands. I like having good suits and an easy rebid in diamonds (after a 1NT response), and would open 1♡ on all three. *You* might not open the first or even the second hand, but I certainly hope you would not pass the 5-4-4-0 hand.

Here are some other distributions where the layout of the two "other suits" makes a difference:

Excellent	Not as Good
4-4-4-1	4-4-3-2
5-5-3-0	5-5-2-1
6-3-3-1	6-3-2-2
6-4-3-0	6-4-2-1
7-3-3-0	7-3-2-1

6 – 4 is Worth More

When your 6-4 hand includes an attractive 6-card major, some modest hands are too good to make a weak 2-bid.

If the 6-card suit becomes trumps, the 4-card suit will often produce an extra trick. Therefore, adding a point for a 6-4 hand is totally reasonable. If you hold 9 HCP, once you add that 1 point to the 9 HCP + a 6-card suit + a 4-card suit, the total is 20, and you should open at the one level.

♠ 7 2   ♡ A Q 10 8 4 3   ◇ 5   ♣ K 9 8 5
9 HCP + 6 hearts + 4 clubs +1 (6-4 hand) = 20.
Open 1♡. You have too much offense to open 2♡, and with two quick tricks, enough defense to open a one bid. In practice, even experts sometimes go wrong and miss games with hands like this by opening a weak 2-bid, because they had "only 9 points."

♠ K Q 10 9 5 4   ♡ 5 3   ◇ A 10 9 6   ♣ 6
Open 1♠, not 2♠. With the high cards and wealth of intermediates in the two long suits, I would upgrade this hand to 10 HCP. Add a point for a nice 6-4 hand, and you are up to 21 with this "much too strong to preempt" hand.

♠ A K 6 4 3 2   ♡ Q 3   ◇ 7 6 4 3   ♣ 6
Open 2♠, not 1♠. Because of a dubious heart holding and very weak diamonds, no upgrades for this hand.

♠ A K Q 10 7 4   ♡ 7 3   ◇ 7 6 4 3   ♣ 6
Open 1♠, not 2♠. Your diamonds still don't sparkle, but **always add a point for an excellent long suit.**

Too Strong to Open Three
(1st or 2nd Seat)

With a 7-card suit headed by the AKQ, open one of your suit, rather than three.

Even if you have nothing else, a suit that will deliver seven tricks off the top is too strong to preempt.

As dealer, you pick up:

♠ 8 6   ♡ 9 2   ♢ 7 5   ♣ A K Q 10 7 5 3

9 HCP + 7 clubs + 2 spades = 18, so this hand does not satisfy the Rule of 20. But, I would open 1♣, intending to rebid that suit for a good long while. If partner has a suitable hand, you'd love to end up in 3NT.

For example:

West	W	E	East
♠ 9 6	1♣	1♠	♠ 8 7 5 4 2
♡ 9 2	2♣	2♡	♡ A K 7 4
♢ 7 5	3♣	3NT	♢ A J 9
♣ A K Q 10 7 5 3			♣ 4

If West makes the mistake of opening 3♣, East has a clear pass, and the good game would be missed.

By the way: If playing "Gambling 3NT," West would open 3NT. This promises a 7-8 card minor headed by the AKQ, while denying an outside ace or king. With the hand above, East would be delighted to pass. With a lesser hand, he would usually bid 4♣ to ask for opener's minor.

Rule of 20 Evaluating Summary

Here is a list of guidelines for evaluating your hand. Adding for upgrades and subtracting for downgrades will always help you make informed decisions as to whether or not to open.

UPGRADES   DOWNGRADES

Honor Cards

more than one ace   more than one queen
                                            more than one jack

honors in your long suit(s)   honors in short suit(s)

honors with other honors   isolated honors

Distribution

long suit   no 5+ card suit

2-suited hand (at least 5-4)   no second suit

singleton or void   flat hand
                                            (4–3–3–3 is worst)

Suit Quality in Long Suit(s)

3+ honors   weak suit(s)

intermediates (10, 9, 8)   no intermediates

an independent 6+ card suit

The Rule of 22

Some players prefer the Rule of 22. It begins the same as the Rule of 20; add the length of your two longest suits to your HCP. However, there is one other addition. You also add your number of quick tricks. If the total is 22 or more, open the bidding.

The Rule of 22 in Action:

1. ♠ Q 5 ♡ Q 7 6 5 ◇ K Q 9 ♣ Q J 7 4
12 HCP + 4 hearts + 4 clubs + 1 quick trick = 21.
Pass.

2. ♠ Q J 10 7 6 ♡ 6 5 3 ◇ A Q J 9 6 ♣ —
10 HCP + 5 spades + 5 diamonds + 1½ quick tricks = 21½.
Not quite enough to open.

3. ♠ K 3 ♡ A J 10 6 5 ◇ 7 5 ♣ K 9 7 4
11 HCP + 5 hearts + 4 clubs + 2 quick tricks = 22.
Open the bidding.

How do I feel about the Rule of 22? Because I believe in the importance of quick tricks, I have no problem with the concept. Both the Rule of 20 and the Rule of 22 will often result in the same conclusion as to whether or not a hand should be opened. In either case, it's important to apply good hand evaluation.

My preference for the Rule of 20 is based on practical considerations. It involves fewer calculations, and mercifully, fractions are not involved.

Tiebreakers for Borderline Hands

Evaluating honor cards and intermediates is the most important adjustment when deciding whether to open. However, for those very experienced players who like to "go the extra mile," here are some factors you *might* wish to consider with a close call.

1. Is there any difference between first and second seat?
Be slightly more aggressive in first seat, because there are *two* unpassed opponents who *might* be eager to bid.

2. Do you have a singleton or void?
Obviously, a 4-4-4-1 hand has more potential than one with 4-4-3-2, just as 5-4-4-0 is better than 5-4-2-2, etc.

3. Length in the majors?
Many authorities believe that major-suit length is significant. Other experts (myself included), argue that if you pass a reasonable hand with length in one or both minors, it will be more difficult to get in later.

4. Are you likely to have a rebid problem?
If the answer is yes, you may decide to avoid the problem by passing a borderline hand. If you will have an easy rebid after partner's expected response, go ahead and open.

Is there any way to anticipate partner's likely response?
  If you open a minor, partner will probably respond in your shorter major.

  If you open a major, partner will probably respond 1NT (or 1♠ after a 1♡ opening bid).

To Open or Not to Open

You are the dealer. Do you open, or do you pass?

1. ♠ J 7 5 4 2   ♡ K   ◇ K Q J   ♣ Q 7 4 2

2. ♠ K Q 10 8   ♡ 6 3   ◇ 7 5 3   ♣ A Q 10 9

3. ♠ K 7 5 4   ♡ J 3   ◇ Q J 5   ♣ K Q 5 3

4. ♠ Q J 10 7 2   ♡ K 5 3   ◇ K J 9 8 6   ♣ —

5. ♠ 4 3   ♡ A Q 10 7 6   ◇ K Q 7 5   ♣ 7 3

6. ♠ A Q   ♡ 10 7 6 5 2   ◇ J 5 4 2   ♣ K Q

7. ♠ J 10 8 4   ♡ A 10 5   ◇ K Q 6 5 4 2   ♣ —

8. ♠ A K J 2   ♡ J 4   ◇ 8 7 6 5 3 2   ♣ Q

9. ♠ A 10 8 7   ♡ A 6 2   ◇ 7 5 4   ♣ A 5 3

10. ♠ A K 4 3   ♡ 3   ◇ A 7 5 4   ♣ 8 6 4 2

11. ♠ Q J 7 3   ♡ J   ◇ Q J 5 4   ♣ A J 4 2

12. ♠ —   ♡ K Q 9 5 3   ◇ A J 10 8   ♣ 7 6 5 3

13. ♠ A J 10 9 6   ♡ 5   ◇ K J 10   ♣ Q 10 9 4

14. ♠ A J 4 3 2   ♡ 5   ◇ K J 2   ♣ Q 5 4 2

To Open or Not to Open

1. ♠ J 7 5 4 2   ♡ K   ◊ K Q J   ♣ Q 7 4 2
At first glance: 12 HCP + 5 spades and 4 clubs = 21.
Pluses: 5-4-3-1 hands have great potential.
Minuses: A singleton king, no aces or intermediates, and two weak, long suits.
In conclusion: Too many minuses.   **Pass**

2. ♠ K Q 10 8   ♡ 6 3   ◊ 7 5 3   ♣ A Q 10 9
At first glance: 11 HCP + 4 spades + 4 clubs = 19.
Pluses: Great intermediates, all your honors are concentrated in the two longest suits, and 2½ quick tricks.
Minuses: 11 HCP.
In conclusion: A lot of pluses.   **Open 1♣**

3. ♠ K 7 5 4   ♡ J 3   ◊ Q J 5   ♣ K Q 5 3
At first glance: 12 HCP + 4 spades + 4 clubs = 20.
Pluses: 12 HCP.
Minuses: No aces or intermediate cards, and only 1½ quick tricks.
In conclusion: The minuses outweigh the pluses.   **Pass**

4. ♠ Q J 10 7 2   ♡ K 5 3   ◊ K J 9 8 6   ♣ —
At first glance: 10 HCP + 5 spades + 5 diamonds = 20.
Pluses: Nice intermediates in your long suits, and a void.
Minuses: 10 HCP with no aces and only 1 quick trick.
In conclusion: Opening with only 1 quick trick is very rare, but this hand has too much potential to pass.

Open 1♠

5. ♠ 4 3 ♡ A Q 10 7 6 ◇ K Q 7 5 ♣ 7 3
At first glance: 11 HCP + five hearts + 4 diamonds = 20.
Pluses: 2½ quick tricks, and all of your honors are concentrated in the two attractive long suits.
Minuses: 2-2 in your other suits, as opposed to 3-1 or 4-0, and only 11 HCP.
In conclusion: Well-located honor cards.   **Open 1♡**

6. ♠ A Q ♡ 10 7 6 5 2 ◇ J 5 4 2 ♣ K Q
At first glance: 12 HCP + five hearts + 4 diamonds = 21.
Pluses: 12 HCP and 2½ quick tricks.
Minuses: Very weak long suits; very strong short suits.
In conclusion: **BAD** location, location, location.   **Pass**

7. ♠ J 10 8 4 ♡ A 10 5 ◇ K Q 6 5 4 2 ♣ —
At first glance: 10 HCP + 6 diamonds + 4 spades = 20.
Pluses: 6-4-3-0 distribution with some intermediates.
Minuses: Only 10 HCP.
In conclusion: Points schmoints!   **Open 1◇**

8. ♠ A K J 2 ♡ J 4 ◇ 8 7 6 5 3 2 ♣ Q
At first glance: 11 HCP + 6 diamonds + 4 spades = 21.
Pluses: A very strong second suit.
Minuses: An emaciated long suit, and very questionable honors in hearts and clubs.
In conclusion: Avoid diamonds that don't sparkle.   **Pass**

9. ♠ A 10 8 7 ♡ A 6 2 ◇ 7 5 4 ♣ A 5 3
At first glance: 12 HCP + 4 spades + 3 hearts = 19.
Pluses: Three aces and some spade intermediates.
Minuses: 4-3-3-3 distribution.
In conclusion: Always open with 3 aces.   **Open 1♣**

10. ♠ A K 4 3   ♡ 3   ◇ A 7 5 4   ♣ 8 6 4 2
At first glance: 11 HCP + 4 spades and 4 diamonds = 19.
Pluses: A 3-suited hand with 3 quick tricks.
Minuses: No intermediates.

In conclusion: Open AK, A (unless 4-3-3-3).   **Open 1◇**

11. ♠ Q J 7 3   ♡ J   ◇ Q J 5 4   ♣ A J 4 2
At first glance: 12 HCP + 4 spades and 4 diamonds = 20.
Pluses: A 3-suited hand.
Minuses: A singleton honor, only one quick trick and no intermediates.

In conclusion: Queens and jacks are overrated.   **Pass**

12. ♠ —   ♡ K Q 9 5 3   ◇ A J 10 8   ♣ 7 6 5 3
At first glance: 10 HCP + 5 hearts + 4 diamonds = 19.
Pluses: A 3-suiter and a void. Honors concentrated in two suits, bolstered by some promising intermediates.
Minuses: Only 10 HCP.

In conclusion: 5-4-4-0 is a great shape.   **Open 1♡**

13. ♠ A J 10 9 6   ♡ 5   ◇ K J 10   ♣ Q 10 9 4
At first glance: 11 HCP + 5 spades and 4 clubs = 20.
Pluses: Exceptional intermediates and 5-4-3-1 distribution.
Minuses: Only 1½ quick tricks.
In conclusion: I love those tens and nines.   **Open 1♠**

14. ♠ A J 4 3 2   ♡ 5   ◇ K J 2   ♣ Q 5 4 2
At first glance: 11 HCP + 5 spades and 4 clubs = 20.
Pluses: 5-4-3-1 distribution.
Minuses: 1½ quick tricks and no intermediates.
In conclusion: Don't open an ugly 11-count.   **Pass**

Too Strong to Preempt?

Your RHO deals and passes.
Do you open, preempt, or pass?

1. ♠ Q 5 ♡ K Q 7 6 5 2 ◇ K J ♣ 7 6 4

2. ♠ 7 5 4 ♡ A Q J 10 9 5 ◇ 5 ♣ K 10 9

3. ♠ Q ♡ Q J ◇ J 4 2 ♣ K Q J 8 7 5 3

4. ♠ K J 8 ♡ 7 6 ◇ 4 ♣ A Q 10 7 6 5 4

5. ♠ 8 5 3 ♡ 6 ◇ A K Q 10 7 6 4 ♣ 6 3

6. ♠ K Q 9 8 7 3 ♡ 6 4 ◇ A 10 9 6 ♣ 2

7. ♠ Q 7 5 4 3 2 ♡ Q 8 3 ◇ K ♣ K J 5

8. ♠ A J 10 9 7 6 5 2 ♡ A 8 5 ◇ 6 4 ♣ —

9. ♠ K Q J 10 9 7 6 2 ♡ K J ◇ 6 4 ♣ 4

Too Strong to Preempt?

1. ♠ Q 5 ♡ K Q 7 6 5 2 ◇ K J ♣ 7 6 4
At first glance: 11 HCP + 6 hearts + 3 clubs = 20.
Pluses: A 6-card suit with 11 HCP.
Minuses: No aces or intermediates, 1½ quick tricks, and questionable holdings in both doubletons.
In conclusion: Too many flaws to open the bidding. Although the three outside honors make this an imperfect preempt, I prefer 2♡ to pass.

Don't open 1♡. **Preempt 2♡**

2. ♠ 7 5 4 ♡ A Q J 10 9 5 ◇ 5 ♣ K 10 9
At first glance: 10 HCP + 6 hearts + 3 spades = 19.
Pluses: A gorgeous heart suit and a singleton, as well as some promising club intermediates.
Minuses: 10 HCP.
In conclusion: You should always upgrade for an independent suit. Once you add one point, you would satisfy the Rule of 20 even if your club holding were K32.

Don't preempt 2♡. **Open 1♡**

3. ♠ Q ♡ Q J ◇ J 4 2 ♣ K Q J 8 7 5 3
At first glance: 12 HCP + 7 clubs + 3 diamonds = 22.
Pluses: 12 HCP, and an excellent long suit.
Minuses: Only 1 quick trick, and all of your honors outside clubs are extremely questionable.
In conclusion: Definitely not worth an opening bid. With so many outside honors, some players would pass.

Don't open 1♣. **Preempt 3♣**

4. ♠ K J 8　♡ 7 6　♢ 4　♣ A Q 10 7 6 5 4

At first glance: 10 HCP + 7 clubs + 3 spades = 20.

Pluses: A nice long suit and a singleton.

Minuses: 10 HCP.

In conclusion: Two quick tricks, and a lot of offense, based on your 7-card suit. That's definitely enough to open the bidding.

Don't preempt 3♣.　　　　**Open 1♣**

5. ♠ 8 5 3　♡ 6　♢ A K Q 10 7 6 4　♣ 6 3

At first glance: 9 HCP + 7 diamonds + 3 spades = 19.

Pluses: Diamonds to die for, and a singleton.

Minuses: 9 HCP.

In conclusion: In first or second seat, don't open three of a suit when your 7-card suit is headed by the AKQ. (If you play "Gambling 3NT," open 3NT.)

Don't preempt 3♢.　　　　**Open 1♢**

6. ♠ K Q 9 8 7 3　♡ 6 4　♢ A 10 9 6　♣ 2

At first glance: 9 HCP + 6 spades + 4 diamonds = 19.

Pluses: 6-4 distribution with all your honors and intermediates concentrated in the two longest suits.

Minuses: 9 HCP.

In conclusion: If your 6-card suit becomes trumps, your 4-card suit is a HUGE asset. That upgrade makes this hand too strong for a weak-two bid.

Don't preempt 2♠.　　　　**Open 1♠**

7. ♠ Q 7 5 4 3 2   ♡ Q 8 3   ◊ K   ♣ K J 5

At first glance: 11 HCP + 6 spades + 3 hearts = 20.

Pluses: A lot of honor cards.

Minuses: A weak long suit, no aces or intermediates, and a dubious diamond honor.

In conclusion: A very flawed hand, and your spade suit is not strong enough to open two.

    Don't bid 1♠ or 2♠.   **Pass**

8. ♠ A J 10 9 7 6 5 2   ♡ A 8 5   ◊ 6 4   ♣ —

At first glance: 9 HCP +8 spades + 3 hearts = 20.

Pluses: Two aces and a void, with an 8-card suit that includes superb intermediates.

Minuses: 9 HCP.

In conclusion: With three first-round controls, you have too much slam potential to preempt.

    Don't preempt 4♠.   **Open 1♠**

9. ♠ K Q J 10 9 7 6 2   ♡ K J   ◊ 6 4   ♣ 4

At first glance: 10 HCP + 8 spades + 2 hearts = 20.

Pluses: An independent 8-card suit.

Minuses: No aces, and a questionable heart holding.

In conclusion: With virtually no defense, and a great suit for offense (only), you are delighted to preempt.

    Don't open 1♠.   **Preempt 4♠**

Part II:

After Deciding to Open a Rule of 20 Hand

Setting The Scene for Part II

I first wrote about the Rule of 20 in 1995, in the book
POINTS SCHMOINTS! Since then I've been asked
hundreds of questions about this topic. The majority of
those have been along the lines of: "I opened based on
the Rule of 20, but didn't know what to do after that.
Marty, what would you have done?"

Accordingly, it was clear that I had to address "how to
follow through after deciding to open a Rule of 20 hand."
That's what "Part II" of this book is all about.

1. **Worth noting:**
All Part II recommendations for "which suit to open" and
rebids are also relevant when you have a slightly stronger
opening bid.

2. **The Law of Total Tricks:**
An invaluable aid for players of all levels in judging
whether or not to bid on in competitive auctions. On the
great majority of hands, you are safe competing to the level
equal to your side's number of trumps.

3. **Reminder regarding "numbers and hyphens:"**
When I use numbers and hyphens to designate a
distribution, such as "4-4-4-1," I am referring to a hand
which contains three 4-card suits, as well as a singleton.
The singleton could be in any one of the four suits.

4. **Reminder on vulnerability for bidding decisions:**
On all hands *in this book*, I suggest taking the same action
whether vulnerable or not.

Which Suit Should You Open?

Suppose that you have decided to open a hand based on the Rule of 20, but are not sure which suit to open. Here are my recommendations, along with examples, and some suggestions as to what to rebid.

4-3-3-3 (4-card major)

Open 1♣, even if the diamonds are much stronger.

♠ K 10 2 ♡ 9 6 5 4 ◇ A K J ♣ Q 3 2
If partner responds 1◇ or 1♠, bid 1NT.
If partner responds 1♡, raise to 2♡.

4-4-3-2 with two 4-card minors

Open your stronger minor.

♠ A Q ♡ K 9 7 ◇ 7 6 4 3 ♣ Q J 10 9   Open 1♣
If partner responds 1◇ or 1♡ or 1♠, bid 1NT.

♠ Q J 9 ♡ 9 6 ◇ A J 10 7 ♣ A 8 4 2   Open 1◇
If partner responds 1♡, rebid 1NT.
If partner responds 1♠, raise to 2♠.

4-4-4-1 with a singleton in a major

Open 1◇, unless you have terrible diamonds and superb clubs – in that case, open 1♣.

♠ 10 ♡ K J 7 5 ◇ J 6 4 2 ♣ A K 9 8   Open 1♣
If partner responds 1◇ or 1♡, raise to two.
If partner responds 1♠, bid 1NT.

4-4-4-1 (continued)

♠ Q 8 7 3   ♡ 9   ◇ K Q 9 8   ♣ K Q 9 8   Open 1◇
If partner responds 1♡, bid 1♠.
If partner responds 1♠, raise to 2♠.

4 diamonds and 5 clubs

If your diamonds are lovely, open 1◇.
If the diamonds don't sparkle, open 1♣.

♠ A 5   ♡ A 6   ◇ 10 5 3 2   ♣ Q J 10 7 4   Open 1♣
If partner responds 1◇, raise to 2◇.
If partner responds 1♡ or 1♠, bid 1NT.

♠ 8 4   ♡ 5 3   ◇ A Q J 9   ♣ A 8 6 4 3   Open 1◇
If partner responds 1♡ or 1♠, bid 2♣.

Two 5-card suits

Open the higher-ranking suit.

♠ 6 5   ♡ 5   ◇ K 10 7 5 4   ♣ A Q J 9 2   Open 1◇
If partner responds 1♡ or 1♠, bid 2♣.

♠ A 4   ♡ Q J 9 8 3   ◇ 5   ♣ K 10 7 5 4   Open 1♡
If partner responds 1♠ or 1NT, bid 2♣.
If partner responds 2◇, bid 2♡ or 3♣
(depending on partnership style).

♠ A J 9 8 3   ♡ 8 3   ◇ 3   ♣ A J 9 8 3   Open 1♠
If partner responds 1NT, bid 2♣.
If partner responds 2◇ or 2♡, bid 2♠ or 3♣
(partnership style).

Which Suit (continued)

6-5 distribution

Because you are not strong enough to reverse, you should open the higher-ranking suit.
However, there are two exceptions:

with 5 spades and 6 clubs, open 1♣; OR

with a very weak 5-card diamond suit and 6 terrific clubs, open 1♣, planning to leave your diamonds at home.

♠ K 7 6 4 2   ♡ 5   ◇ 3   ♣ A Q 10 9 4 3   Open 1♣
If partner responds 1◇ or 1♡, bid 1♠.

♠ 6   ♡ 8   ◇ 7 6 5 3 2   ♣ A K Q 7 5 4   Open 1♣
If partner responds 1♡ or 1♠, bid 2♣.

♠ 8 4   ♡ —   ◇ K Q 9 7 2   ♣ A 10 8 6 3 2   Open 1◇
If partner responds 1♡ or 1♠, bid 2♣.

♠ —   ♡ A Q 10 4 2   ◇ 7 3   ♣ K 9 7 6 4 3   Open 1♡
If partner responds 1♠ or 1NT, bid 2♣.
If partner responds 2◇, bid 2♡ or 3♣
(partnership style).

♠ A K 9 7 2   ♡ 5   ◇ Q 10 9 8 4 3   ♣ 2   Open 1♠
If partner responds 1NT or 2♣, bid 2◇.
If partner responds 2♡, bid 2♠ or 3◇
(partnership style).

Know Your Limits
(Noncompetitive Auctions)

Whenever possible, select a rebid which says loud and clear, "I have a minimum opening bid."

This is often referred to as "limiting your hand."

1. You open 1♣ and partner responds 1◇.

♠ 9 7   ♡ 10 7 5 4   ◇ J   ♣ A K Q J 10 5
Bid 2♣, not 1♡. An "up the line" 1♡ bid would be carrying things too far. You want to tell partner that you have a 6-card suit with just a minimum opening bid. A 1♡ rebid is ambiguous as to strength; it might include as many as 17 or even 18 HCP. It's also true that rebidding your gorgeous club suit describes this hand much better than talking about your emaciated hearts.

2. You open 1♡ and partner responds 1♠.

♠ A 10 4   ♡ K 10 8 6 4   ◇ A 6 5 2   ♣ 3
Bid 2♠, not 2◇. Although partner could have only four spades, you should raise with this hand. Let him know that you have a minimum opening bid with support for his suit.

3. You open 1♣ and partner responds 1◇.

♠ 9 7 6 5   ♡ K J 9   ◇ A J 8   ♣ K J 4
Bid 1NT, not 1♠. Tell partner that you have a minimum, balanced opening bid. A 1♠ rebid could include 17-18 HCP and/or a very distributional hand. **With 4-3-3-3, bid notrump ASAP.**

Rebidding After Finding a Fit

Once you find a major-suit fit, be aggressive with good distribution.

1. You open 1♠ and partner raises to 2♠.

♠ A 8 7 6 5 4 2   ♡ 9   ◇ A J 10 8   ♣ 3
Bid 4♠. Anything less would be cowardly. With a 10-card fit, (your seven and partner's three), The LAW of Total Tricks says that you should not hesitate to contract for 10 tricks. After partner's raise, this hand is so good that even if his only useful card is a diamond honor, your chances of making 4♠ are excellent.

2. You open 1♡ and partner makes a limit raise of 3♡.

♠ A 6 3   ♡ K 9 5 4 2   ◇ K 10 9 7 3   ♣ —
Bid 4♡. If most of partner's strength is in clubs, you might not make 4♡, but with this shape, you're delighted to be in game. Marty Sez: When you open 1♡ or 1♠ and partner makes a limit raise, do not pass if you have a singleton or void.

3. | You | Partner |
    | --- | --- |
    | 1♠ | 1NT |
    | 2♡ | 3♡ |
    | ??? | |

♠ 9 8 6 5 3   ♡ A Q 10 4 2   ◇ 9   ♣ A 8
Bid 4♡, whether or not 1NT was forcing. On this auction, your fifth heart is worth its weight in gold.

Competitive Bidding Guidelines

Principles for opener when deciding whether to make a free bid in a competitive auction.

Once your RHO does not pass, any bid you make is "free" because partner will get a chance to bid even if you pass.

1. As usual, HCP are not the key. If you have something worth saying, go ahead and say it. Playing the "waiting game" can come back to haunt you. On the other hand, you don't have to bid just because it's your turn.

2. Shape is the name of the game. Your holding in the opponent's suit is crucial. The shorter you are, the harder you should try to take action.

With a singleton or void, strive to bid.
A doubleton is inconclusive, so consider other factors.
With 3+ cards in their suit, only make *obvious* bids.

3. As usual, be more aggressive when nonvulnerable. However, being vulnerable should not stop you from competing with a worthwhile hand.

4. Be aggressive (but not suicidal) at the one or two level. You'll never have a cheaper opportunity to bid.
At higher levels, think twice before making a free bid.

5. Whether or not you have a fit, the quality of your long suit(s) is VERY important. In addition to looking at honor cards, don't forget to consider the intermediates. If partner doesn't have any support, your intermediate cards can make all the difference in the world.

6. Everyone loves a fit. Therefore:
    A. Be aggressive when *your* side has a fit.
    B. Be aggressive when *their* side has a fit.
    C. "Support with support."
    D. Follow The LAW of Total Tricks.

7. "5-5, come alive."
If you have not yet found a fit, be eager to let partner know
about your second suit – who knows, you might uncover a
great fit. If you don't show your other suit, the fit may be
gone forever. If the auction allows you to show your
second suit at the two level, bid it.

8. Don't neglect your responsibility to balance.
A bonanza might be just around the corner.

You	LHO	Partner	RHO
1 suit	overcall	Pass	Pass
???			

Having a Rule of 20 hand should not stop you from
balancing, except when you have length in the opponent's
suit. Partner may have made a "trap" pass, based on length
and strength in the opponent's suit. That is quite likely
when you opened light and two players passed. Partner is
counting on you to give him a second chance. He'll
usually be delighted if you can balance with a double,
allowing him to make a penalty pass and kick butt.

However, when considering a balancing double at a low
level, "avoid with a void," but be eager with a singleton.
Having even one trump can allow you to lead *through* the
overcaller. Voids are assets on offense, but liabilities on
defense. If you are void in LHO's suit, try to bid rather
than double.

To Bid or Not to Bid

You are always South, as indicated by "???" Keep in mind the competitive principles discussed on pages 47-48.

In the examples that feature a 1NT response to a major, the answer should be the same whether or not you are playing 1NT Forcing.

South	West	North	East
1♡	Pass	1NT	2♣
???			

1. ♠ K 10 6 ♡ K J 5 4 3 2 ◇ A ♣ 5 4 2
Pass. Don't be seduced by your sixth heart. With three cards in East's suit, and a heart suit that's full of holes, silence is golden.

2. ♠ K 10 6 ♡ K J 10 9 8 7 ◇ A ♣ 5 4 2
Bid 2♡. With a suit guaranteed to deliver at least four tricks with hearts as trumps, you're delighted to rebid your 6-card suit.

South	West	North	East
1♡	Pass	1NT	2◇
???			

3. ♠ K 10 6 ♡ K J 5 4 3 2 ◇ A ♣ 5 4 2
Bid 2♡. Now that your singleton is in the opponent's suit, you're unwilling to risk defending at the two level.

South	West	North	East
South	*West*	*North*	*East*
1♡	Pass	1NT	2♠
???			

4. ♠7 ♡A8642 ◇A3 ♣Q9872
Bid 3♣. Partner's 1NT response denied four spades, so you know that the opponents have at least nine spades. Your side must have a fit. If partner hates both of your suits, he must have a long diamond suit, and can bid 3◇.

5. ♠J 10 3 ♡A Q 10 4 2 ◇K 7 6 5 3 ♣—
Pass. With the club void and two tens, this hand looked more promising than the previous one. However, the 2♠ overcall changed everything. Your spade holding opens up the possibility of three fast losers if your side takes the bid. If partner also has three spades, neither side may have a fit.

Keep in mind that your pass does not necessarily end the auction. Partner probably has a lot of clubs. If he balances with 3♣, you will bid 3◇ and hope that partner has at least three of those.

6. ♠— ♡K 9 7 5 3 ◇A 10 8 4 ♣A 10 5 2
With a spade void, pass is out of the question. However, because this is not an up-the-line situation, you can't simply bid your cheaper minor and expect partner to correct to diamonds unless he has at least six. The only answer is for your partnership to define opener's double after partner's 1NT response as takeout (alertable), not penalties. This is approach is logical and flexible, and experience has shown it to be an excellent convention. **At low levels, treat very few doubles as "penalty."**

South	West	North	East
1♡	Pass	1NT	2♠
???			

7. ♠ 7 2 ♡ A 7 5 4 3 2 ◇ 6 ♣ A Q 10 9

Bid 3♣ with this nice 6-4 hand, which includes 2½ quick tricks, and all your honors in your two longest suits. The only question is whether to rebid hearts or introduce clubs. The answer is suit quality; your clubs are chunky while your hearts are not.

South	West	North	East
1◇	1♡	Dbl	2♡
???			

8. ♠ 7 6 5 3 ♡ A 5 ◇ K J 10 7 4 ♣ K 3

Bid 2♠. Your spades are lousy, and your hand is nothing to write home about. However, after partner promised four spades with his Negative Double, it would be foolish to not compete to the two level in your known 8-card fit.

9. ♠ 8 5 ♡ A 5 ◇ A 8 7 6 4 3 ♣ K 9 7

Pass. This definitely started out as a better hand than the previous one. It's also true that you expect to have a fit. Unfortunately, a bid would take you to the three level, and you're not even sure which minor you belong in. Partner could have a singleton diamond with club length. He also knows about their fit, and will be eager to balance.

South	West	North	East
1♣	Pass	1NT	2♡
???			

10. ♠ A 10 4   ♡ 5   ♢ K Q 8   ♣ Q 9 6 5 4 3

Bid 3♣. Your suit lacks quality, but partner can't be short in clubs after he bypassed the other three suits. When each side has a known fit, selling out at the the two level can't be right.

11. ♠ Q J 5   ♡ Q J 3   ♢ K Q   ♣ Q J 6 4 2

Pass. Yuck, what a disgusting hand! On the surface, this hand adds to 22 (14 HCP + 5 clubs + 3 spades). In reality, with no aces or intermediates, and only one quick trick, you should bid again only when forced to do so.

South	West	North	East
1♢	Pass	1♠	2♡
???			

12. ♠ 6 5   ♡ 6   ♢ A 10 9 8 5   ♣ A Q 10 9 8

Bid 3♣. Great distribution, great intermediates, and a club suit worth talking about. Three good reasons to forge ahead to the three level.

13. ♠ K   ♡ Q J   ♢ K Q J 3 2   ♣ Q 7 6 5 3

Pass. You don't usually think of 5-5 hands with 14 HCP as Rule of 20 opening bids, but this hand is ugly as sin. You have terrible holdings in both major suits and no aces. Straining to show your other minor with a free bid at the three level makes no sense.

South	West	North	East
1♢	Pass	1NT	2♠
???			

14. ♠ 7 5 ♡ A 4 ♢ A K 8 5 4 ♣ 5 4 3 2

Bid 3♣. Once partner bypasses hearts and spades and fails to support diamonds, his 13 cards invariably include at least four clubs. You are guaranteed to have a fit in one (or both) minors.

South	West	North	East
1♠	2♢	2♠	3♢
???			

15. ♠ J 10 6 5 4 2 ♡ K Q 7 2 ♢ A 5 ♣ 7

Bid 3♠. Your six spades and partner's three totals nine, so follow The LAW of Total Tricks and compete to the three level. Declarer's 4-card side suit is usually worth an extra trick.

16. ♠ A K J 7 6 ♡ A 5 2 ♢ 7 4 ♣ 7 5 4

Pass. You have a nice, "normal" opening bid, but no reason to bid on to the three level. Hands like this should become automatic – just follow The LAW. It's also true that 5-3-3-2 is a horrible distribution for developing additional tricks.

17. ♠ A 10 8 6 5 3 ♡ 2 ♢ 4 ♣ K Q 10 9 4

Bid 4♠. Once partner promises support, you must be in game. 6-5 hands with a guaranteed fit always re-evaluate fantastically well.

South	West	North	East
1♣	Pass	1◇	1♡
???			

18. ♠ A K J 9 ♡ K 4 ◇ 6 3 ♣ 10 8 7 5 3

Bid 1♠. At the one level, there are no reverses and you don't need extra strength for a free bid. You have fabulous spades, and a well-placed ♡K, so why not bid?

19. ♠ J 5 4 3 ♡ J 8 4 ◇ A 7 4 ♣ A Q J

Pass. These spades are ugly, as is your distribution. Your heart holding is also mediocre. If partner has spades, he is welcome to bid them.

20. ♠ K 10 8 ♡ 2 ◇ A K J ♣ 8 7 6 5 4 3

Bid 2◇. You don't usually support a minor suit when you have your own 6-card suit. However, with an anemic club suit that would be more useful for poker, let partner know how fond you are of diamonds.

South	West	North	East
1◇	Pass	1♡	2♠
???			

21. ♠ 8 7 6 2 ♡ 2 ◇ K Q J 10 9 8 ♣ A 4

Pass. Lovely diamonds, but with length in their suit and shortness in partner's, avoid a free bid at the three level.

22. ♠ 4 ♡ 7 2 ◇ A Q J 10 9 5 2 ♣ K 5 3

Bid 3◇. Not only did you inherit an additional diamond, but you like having a singleton in the opponent's suit.

South	West	North	East
1♢	1♠	2♡	3♠
???			

23. ♠ 2   ♡ 9   ♢ A J 10 8 7   ♣ A 8 6 5 4 3

Bid 4♣. Whether or not you would have opened this shapely hand is not relevant *now*. You've got to let partner know about your very long other suit. If you're nervous about making a free bid at the four level with only 9 HCP, keep in mind that partner's 2♡ bid promised 10 points, and because they have a fit, you must have one as well.

24. ♠ 7 6 4   ♡ 6   ♢ A K 9 8 5 4 3   ♣ K 4

When this hand was played in a national tournament, the expert holding the hand passed, because he didn't want to make a free bid at the four level with 10 HCP and a singleton in partner's suit. However, when partner then bid 4♡, he was faced with "The lady or the tiger" – should he pass, or correct to 5♢? He guessed to pass, which was a disaster when his side finished down one in 4♡; cold for a diamond slam. Partner held:

♠ 9   ♡ A J 9 7 5 3   ♢ J 6 2   ♣ A Q 9

If our expert had guessed to bid 5♢ over 4♡, he would have done better, but he would not have felt good if partner had a terrific long heart suit with a singleton diamond.

Of course, the moral is very clear. Because opener had something to tell his partner about, he should have rebid his diamonds at the four level while he had the chance. If he had, he would have been *well-placed* to abide by any decision that partner might have made.

South	West	North	East
1◇	Pass	1♡	1♠
???			

25. ♠ A 7 3 ♡ 4 3 ◇ K Q J 2 ♣ Q 5 4 3

Pass. You don't have to make a free bid of 1NT just because you have a spade stopper.

26. ♠ K J 9 ♡ 4 3 ◇ A J 10 8 ♣ K 9 8 3

Bid 1NT. Here you have prospects of two spade stoppers as well as a fistful of intermediates.

27. ♠ 6 4 ♡ K Q 6 ◇ K 9 6 3 2 ♣ A 5 4

Bid 2♡. Opener must be willing to raise with 3-card support, even though partner might have a 4-card suit. If playing the excellent convention, "Support Doubles," you'd double to show that you had exactly three hearts.

28. ♠ K 4 3 ♡ 2 ◇ A J 7 6 5 4 ♣ K 3 2

Bid 2◇. Your diamonds are not gorgeous, but you are willing to show them off at the two level.

South	West	North	East
1♣	Pass	1♠	2◇
???			

29. ♠ K Q 9 4 ♡ 7 4 3 ◇ — ♣ A J 10 9 4 3

Bid 3♠. When partner responded in spades, the value of this hand skyrocketed. Having a void in the opponent's suit is a tremendous asset. These are the kind of hands that often result in making game or slam without many HCP.

South	West	North	East
1♠	2♢	Pass	Pass
???			

30. ♠ A K 8 6 4 3   ♡ 10 7 6   ♢ 6   ♣ A 7 5

Double, don't bid 2♠. You should give partner a chance for a penalty pass, which is probably what he has. The upside for double is a lucrative penalty against 2♢ doubled. On these kinds of auctions, unless it's out of the question, you should be eager to reopen with a double.

31. ♠ A 8 7 6 3   ♡ A 9 5   ♢ 7 3   ♣ K J 10

Double. The chances of partner having a penalty pass would be much greater if you had a singleton diamond. Nevertheless, you should give him a chance. If all he has is a "nothing special" weak hand, you are prepared for any suit he might bid.

32. ♠ 10 9 8 6 4 3   ♡ 8 6   ♢ —   ♣ A K Q 7 6

Bid 3♣. Partner *must* be sitting with a diamond stack, but doubling with this distribution would be presumptuous. If partner's diamonds are really fabulous, you will offer an apology – without any regrets.

33. ♠ A 10 8 4 3   ♡ K 10 5 4   ♢ A 4 3   ♣ 7

Pass. You correctly opened your upgradable 5-4-3-1 hand based on length in the majors, promising intermediates, and 2½ quick tricks. However, you can't expect partner to have a trap pass when you hold ♢A 4 3. Partner didn't raise spades or make a negative double, so either he has nothing, or he has clubs. In either case, it's time to call it a day.

Also Worth Noting

1. Respect partner's forcing bids.

1♡	3◇	3♠	Pass
???			

♠ 6 2 ♡ K 10 8 5 3 ◇ A 5 ♣ A 4 3 2

Bid 3NT. You have no idea where your nine tricks are coming from, but partner's new suit is forcing, so you should admit to your diamond stopper.

♠ A ♡ A Q 7 5 4 2 ◇ J 3 2 ♣ 8 6 3

Bid 4♡. If partner passes, you'll be very nervous before you see the dummy – but what else could you do?

2. Some Rule of 20 hands warrant removing partner's penalty double.

1♠	1NT	Dbl	Pass
???			

♠ J 7 5 4 2 ♡ 7 ◇ A 10 9 ♣ K Q J 9

Bid 2♣. Defending 1NT doubled with an expected spade lead – no thanks.

1♣	1♡	1♠	Pass
2♣	2♡	Dbl	Pass
???			

♠ 9 2 ♡ — ◇ Q 10 9 6 ♣ A K 10 8 7 5 4

Bid 3♣. Partner's double is definitely for penalties, but you definitely have no interest in defending 2♡ doubled with a hand that is screaming "offense."

Easy Does It

Once your partnership has agreed to open light based on the Rule of 20, responder must avoid insisting on game with a borderline hand. If the hand is flawed, responder should prefer to invite, even when he has "an opening bid opposite an opening bid." Unless opener promises extra values, a flexible invitation is recommended whether or not you do find a fit.

On the following hands, you are the responder (North).

South	West	North	East
1♣	Pass	1♠	Pass
2♠	Pass	???	

1. ♠ K Q J 7 4   ♡ J 6 2   ◇ K J   ♣ Q 6 5
Bid 3♠, not 4♠. If opener has a minimum opening bid and declines your invitation, you will have no regrets. You have no aces or intermediates and too many jacks.

South	West	North	East
1♡	Pass	1♠	Pass
2◇	Pass	???	

2. ♠ A K J 7 4   ♡ 6 4 3   ◇ 9 2   ♣ K J 3
Bid 3♡, not 4♡. You have no high cards in partner's two suits. Give opener some leeway by only inviting game. If he has more than a minimum opening bid, he'll be happy to accept your invitation.

3. ♠ J 7 5 3 2   ♡ 7   ◇ A K   ♣ K J 6 4 2
Bid 2NT, not 3NT or 3♣. Beware the misfit.

Highly Recommended

Hardcover Books by Marty Bergen

MARTY SEZ	$17.95
MARTY SEZ - VOLUME 2	$17.95
POINTS SCHMOINTS!	$19.95
More POINTS SCHMOINTS!	$19.95
Schlemiel...Schlimazel? Mensch (not a bridge book)	$14.95

·· UNPRECEDENTED OFFER ··

If your purchase of Marty's hardcover books exceeds $25, mention this book and receive a free copy of any one of Marty's softcover books. Personalized autographs available upon request.

Special Discount!

365 Bridge Hands with Expert Analysis
$13.95   only $5

Bridge Cruises with Marty Bergen

For more information, call 1-800-367-9980

Highly Recommended

Softcover Books by Marty Bergen

Buy 2, get 1 (equal or lesser price) for half price

To Open or Not to Open: *Featuring the Rule of 20*	$6.95
Better Rebidding with Bergen	$7.95
Understanding 1NT Forcing	$5.95
Hand Evaluation: Points, Schmoints!	$7.95
Introduction to Negative Doubles	$6.95
Negative Doubles	$9.95
Better Bidding With Bergen 1 – *Uncontested Auctions*	$11.95
Better Bidding With Bergen 2 – *Competitive Bidding*	$11.95
Marty's Reference book on Conventions ~~$9.95~~	$7.00

Books by Eddie Kantar

A Treasury of Bridge Bidding Tips	$11.95
Take Your Tricks (Declarer Play)	$12.95
Defensive Tips for Bad Card Holders	$12.95

Now Available

CDs by Larry Cohen

Play Bridge With Larry Cohen
An exciting opportunity to play question-and-answer
with a 17-time national champion. "One of the best
products to come along in years. Easy-to-use. Suitable
for every player who wishes to improve his scores."

Day 1	~~$29.95~~	$26
Day 2	~~$29.95~~	$26
Day 3	~~$29.95~~	$26

Books by Larry Cohen

To Bid or Not to Bid - The Law of Total Tricks $12.95

Following the Law - The Total Tricks Sequel $12.95

CDs by Kit Woolsey

Cavendish 2000:

Day 1	~~$29.95~~	$26
Days 2-3	~~$29.95~~	$26

Software by Fred Gitelman

Bridge Master 2000   ~~$59.95~~ $48
"Best software ever created for improving your
declarer play."

· · FREE SHIPPING ON ALL SOFTWARE · ·
(in the U.S.)

One-On-One with Marty

Why not improve your bridge with an experienced, knowledgeable teacher? Enjoy a private bridge lesson with Marty Bergen. You choose the format and topics, including Q&A, conventions, bidding, and cardplay.

Marty is available for lessons via phone and e-mail. Beginners, intermediates, and advanced players will all benefit from his clear and helpful teaching style.

For further information, please call the number below, or e-mail Marty at: mbergen@mindspring.com

ORDERING INFORMATION

To place your order, call Marty toll-free at
1-800-386-7432
all major credit cards are welcome

Or send a check or money order (U.S. currency), to:

Marty Bergen
9 River Chase Terrace
Palm Beach Gardens, FL 33418-6817

Please include $3 postage and handling for each order.

Postage is FREE (in U.S.) if your order includes
any CD or copy of Marty's hardcover books.